Foreword

Eight years ago, when I first opened my restaurant, The Fat Duck, in Bray, I was so busy that on Saturday mornings my first two children would come with me to work. Jack and Jessica, then four and two, would sit on a work surface, their legs dangling far off the floor, and watch what was going on in the kitchen. Eventually I got them involved. They would shell borlotti beans for me and taste sauces or look at samples of raw fish to check them for freshness. They began to have fun and it turned those Saturday mornings from being a bore for them, into an occasion we could all look forward to.

It made me realise that it's never too early to get children involved in the preparation of food. True, my kids started out in a commercial kitchen which can be a very different place from the room at home where most of us cook. Still, the same principles apply. By getting children to join in they can gain a greater understanding of how different dishes are made. They can learn where foods comes from – out of the ground or the sea or from an animal – and they can grasp the importance of the seasons.

But the experience goes much further than that. By trusting them, under proper supervision, to use knives for chopping or to work with flame at the cooker, the kitchen can become a place where children build their confidence. It provides a great work-out for their senses – not just of taste and smell, but of touch and hearing and sight too. And it breaks down the barriers between adults and children; if you've all been involved in cooking the food you're about to eat, you all end up on the same level when you sit down at the table.

That's why I am so pleased to introduce *More than cooking*. It's an invaluable guide for carers and parents alike on how to introduce young children to the pleasures of cooking. In an age when magazine recipes constantly claim to offer 'simplicity' – when all they really offer are horribly short instructions – it's great to have a publication that understands the importance of passing on proper kitchen skills. In *More than cooking,* you'll find brilliant information on the value of advance preparation, accurate measuring and food-handling, and much more besides.

And, of course, there are some great recipes. My favourites? The 'above-ground' and 'below-ground' soups. And the strawberry granita looks like the kind of thing my lot would adore. Whatever you decide to cook from these pages, I do hope that your time in the kitchen really is about more than cooking.

Heston Blumenthal is chef-proprietor of Michelin-starred restaurant The Fat Duck and author of *Family food*, published by Michael Joseph.

Contents

Why cooking with young children is important

Cooking stimulates the hearts and minds of young children and is a most loved and effective activity. From a familiar, unthreatening starting point, it not only teaches a wide variety of social and physical skills, but also involves numerous learning experiences ranging from the mathematical to the linguistic, the scientific to the creative.

So powerful is the influence of cooking upon young children that it often leaves pleasant memories which endure for decades. Many adults recall making cakes, bread or sandwiches as children and sharing and eating them with friends.

A single well-planned and properly supervised cooking session can achieve many of the social and intellectual aims which have long been recognised as desirable by experienced nursery practitioners. Cooking with young children – as opposed to cooking *for* them – quickly demonstrates another truth: that early years skills are often underestimated and that even small children are capable of performing the majority of food preparation and cooking jobs without any danger to themselves. While safety must always be a major consideration – protection against scalding being particularly important – tasks such as chopping fruit can safely be delegated to children after a little common-sense guidance. And there are many benefits. When children help to prepare food and cook, they are obliged to cooperate, collaborate, take turns, share and hypothesise about outcomes. The process of helping leads to improvements in manipulative ability and hand – eye coordination. Afterwards there is an opportunity to record and report: verbally, in writing or through drawings.

In every step, too, there is something to be learned. There are mathematical concepts behind the counting out of spoonfuls, the reading of weighing scales, the use of measuring jugs and the division of portions into halves or quarters. There is science in the manipulation of liquids, powders and solids and in changes of state – freezing, melting, toasting, the raising of bread. There are aesthetic lessons to be found in the colours, textures and smells of the basic ingredients. And in all those numbers, colours and names (50 grams, black pepper, coriander, pestle and mortar, nutmeg) verbal skills are also developed.

During cooking activities children will learn about the relationship between the things that grow and the things they see on the dining table. 'Above-ground' and 'below-ground' vegetable soups, for instance are created from a combination of root crops – carrots, potatoes and parsnips, say – or leaf crops such as cabbage, lettuce and celery [see page 21].

Cooking with young children has an additional importance as it encourages children to eat meals sitting down together at a table. This is a custom abandoned by many households today as eating is often done on the move or in front of the TV, which can reduce family cohesion. Of equal importance is the need to encourage healthy eating and to discourage convenience foods. Children are much more prepared to eat unfamiliar food if they have helped to cook it. In this way their range of acceptable foods can be extended beyond the level of fish fingers, burgers and chips.

Cooking with young children is a wonderful way to introduce new experiences which can add to their knowledge in all sorts of ways.

Practicalities

Health and safety

Before undertaking any activity which involves food, children must be reminded to wash their hands and wear protective clothing – such as aprons – and must be told not to lick their fingers or spoons, at least not until the end of the session! They obviously need to be told how to handle correctly, safely and effectively tools such as knives, graters, corers, zesters and whisks.

Children need to be made aware of any heat source involved and the care involved in dealing with it. Only the adult must handle hot receptacles, using oven gloves, and the children must not be allowed to handle cooked items or containers until they have cooled.

Equipment and preparation

An attractive designated area for cooking activities is ideal. This should be accessible and well equipped with aprons or overalls and tables, as well as a cupboard and a drawer containing:

- a variety of different-sized bowls
- wooden and metal spoons
- cake and tart tins
- baking trays
- measures
- scales
- scissors
- whisks
- graters
- a pestle and mortar
- a lemon squeezer
- baking paper
- paper and foil cases
- pizza tins
- saucepans
- woks
- cookery books
- recipe cards
- labelled containers of basic ingredients.

Other items can be used by the children and the adult together, such as electric mixers and food processors, bread makers, juicers, knives, microwave ovens and cookers.

Throughout, it is important to use tools which work but also to instil in the children a healthy respect and understanding of their potential hazards.

Adults need to plan for all the children to participate in cooking activities, encouraging both boys and girls to take part in an early years setting or school. There should be access for children with special educational needs or disabilities. The equipment may need to be adapted, for example, when cooking with visually impaired children. The resources, utensils and ingredients should also reflect the breadth of children's cultural and religious experiences, as should related resources in puzzles, books, artefacts and the home corner.

Cooking across the curriculum

In each of the four UK countries (England, Scotland, Wales and Northern Ireland), the curriculum for young children has been split into separate areas, and practitioners identify children's learning in terms of these curriculum areas for planning purposes. Cooking with young children is an excellent vehicle for fulfilling many of the aims laid out in these curriculum areas including those identified below. (Note that the titles for each curriculum area differ slightly across the UK, although they cover similar themes. The following headings attempt to encompass these different titles rather than refer exclusively to those in, say, England or Scotland. The principles remain the same across the UK.)

Personal, social and emotional development

Given the opportunity for involvement in cooking activities with adults and peers, children respond well to the challenge. They willingly take on real responsibilities for planning, setting up, clearing away, serving snacks and sharing the results of their work. They learn to respect themselves and others, to value and celebrate food and the eating habits of other cultures. They develop a sense of community and of pride in their own achievements.

In all this the adults involved serve as important role models, capable of exerting much influence through the excitement and enthusiasm they generate. For the children, independence and self-confidence can be developed by providing a well-defined area incorporating a storage system which gives the children access to ingredients and equipment.

A cooking activity often involves several processes and demands high levels of involvement, attention and concentration. It demands the ability to work harmoniously in a group composed of both children and adults as well as a preparedness to take turns and share fairly.

It is essential for adults to know when to intervene, guide and support, while encouraging the children to solve problems and assist each other. Adults must also be alert to children's strengths and weaknesses and must give them plenty of opportunities to practise more difficult skills. Sharing food and recipes in an early years setting or school is a good way of developing relationships with parents and strengthening the positive impressions children have of their own cultures and those of others.

Language, literacy and communication

Cooking provides a meaningful way of developing communication and language skills in children. To set up a collaborative cooking session, they need to interact with adults and peers. The practitioner comments on the experiences they are having, introducing new concepts and language, for example: 'You are squeezing, [mixing, whisking, blending, chopping, peeling]'.

Children need to listen carefully to instructions covering an ongoing process or about what to do next. They use unfamiliar equipment and ingredients and are constantly trying out new vocabulary and learning to categorise food, for example whether a tomato is a fruit or a vegetable, or how 'peas' are related to 'mangetout'.

They must sort, group and sequence their activities ('First we wash our hands, then we put on our aprons, next we weigh the flour. After that we add the sugar'). Adults can encourage the children to report on their activity, to record it graphically and share it with others. They can also help children to anticipate and predict the outcome of their cooking activity coherently, then plan for the next stage and use talk to organise, sequence and clarify their thinking and ideas.

Displays can be set up in a setting to remind children of what they have experienced, using their own work, photographs and books. Story and picture books related to growing, cooking and eating food can provide a familiar link with the cooking activity [see page 30].

Songs and rhymes can also be used – such as:

Chop, chop, choppity chop,
Chop at the bottom and chop at the top.
What you have left you put in the pot.
Chop, chop, choppity chop.
or
Mix a pancake, stir a pancake,
Pour it in the pan.
Fry a pancake, toss a pancake,
Catch it if you can.

Knowledge and understanding of the world around us
Mathematical and scientific development

Mathematical and scientific experiences abound in all cooking activities.

The need for numbers and quantities generally emerges right at the beginning of most cooking exercises. How many spoons full of sugar do we need? What weight of flour should be placed upon the scales? How many millilitres of water should we pour into the standard measuring jug? And for these procedures a mathematical vocabulary is immediately required: more or less; too many, too few; greater or smaller; heavier or lighter.

At a later stage in the activity further concepts may come into play. The concept of addition and subtraction, for example, in deciding how many tarts will fit into the tart tin. The concept of division in deciding how many tarts will be available for each child when they are cooked. The children should be encouraged to estimate the answers to such problems and then check to see if they are right.

Moreover, the more advanced concept of fractions is easily grasped by children if they are physically involved in dividing an apple or a cake – first into two pieces, then four, and so on. If this is accompanied by the use of the correct vocabulary by the practitioner or parent – 'cut it into two halves, four quarters', etc – the children rapidly pick up the language and use it in their play at the dough table, the home corner and the sand tray.

Shape and size – crucial to mathematics – can also be explored. In examining the shapes of biscuits, for example, these shapes can be judged against cutters, tins and containers, with opportunities to compare sizes and weights.

Children also learn about sequencing when following a recipe – they may be told, for example: 'Before we make the soup we must peel the potatoes'. The passage of time is another important factor which they learn when they set the timer for the correct number of minutes to cook their cakes.

All this use of scales, measures and timers helps the children to recognise written numerals. They can be additionally encouraged to do so by number rhymes, many of which involve food: *'Five currant buns'*, for example, or *'One potato, two potato'*.

Cooking activities are as rich in scientific phenomena as they are in mathematical concepts. The children observe liquids and solids and see them freeze, boil and melt. They are introduced to other changes of state, as when dough becomes pastry or when egg whites are whisked to create the foam of a meringue.

They see what are chemical reactions in action, such as when bicarbonate of soda or yeast gives off carbon dioxide to create the voids in bread or cakes. If fresh yeast is mixed with the water, the chemical reaction can be made quite explicit by the resultant bubbling and fizzing. And when the cake mixture rises to become the finished cake, the children become familiar with the idea of expansion. They also see how ingredients combine and change when liquidised, grated, cooked or frozen.

It is important for the adult to exploit these changes by encouraging children to hypothesise on the outcome of a cooking procedure and to ask them open-ended questions which can help them think things through, for example: 'What would happen here if...?', or 'What else can we try?'

The children should also be encouraged to tell each other what they have found out, to speculate on future findings and describe their experiences.

Interaction with the wider world
Visits to farms, garden centres, markets and shops introduce children to fresh ingredients such as fruit and vegetables to use in their food preparation. They should be encouraged to explore these and other ingredients with all their senses and to discuss their findings.

Foods with similar or different properties can be collected, for example vegetables which grow above the ground and those which grow below [see pages 21 and 25 for recipes]. Similarly, the children can compare sweet with sour foods and juices, hard with soft fruits and fruits bearing small seeds with those carrying large stones.

First-hand experience of growing fruit and vegetables – digging up potatoes, picking fruit to eat raw or to cook – are all exciting and meaningful experiences for children which may engender a life-long love of gardening, cooking and healthy eating. Alternatives include visits to local allotments or the garden of a friendly grandparent. On a smaller scale, a tray of cress can provide interest and excitement when it is seen to germinate and grow – and is then used to make sandwiches with egg or cream cheese.

Practitioners can talk to children about the importance of choosing healthy foods and can make them aware that good practices in eating and hygiene can contribute to good health, energy and growth.

In a setting or school, festivals, birthdays and other events present wonderful opportunities to introduce and prepare special celebratory foods associated with a range of cultures and religions – for example pancakes with fresh lemon and orange juice on Shrove Tuesday, stir-fry vegetables, rice and prawn crackers for Chinese New Year, miniature puddings and mince pies at Christmas, samosas, dal, cucumber raita and poori breads for Eid and Diwali, potato latkes for Hanukkah and hot cross buns at Easter. Recipes for most of these appear later in the book [see pages 17–29].

It is important to involve parents in such activities, to use their knowledge and expertise and share the food produced with families. Successful occasions include family picnics and lunches for grandparents when the children are responsible for helping to prepare the food and for serving it to visitors. This gives them a feeling of pride and achievement and is very popular with grandparents – and often great-grandparents.

History
Grandparents and great-grandparents can also be helpful by communicating a sense of history to children. Over the past 50 years in the UK – in the lifetime of most children's grandparents and great-grandparents – there have been profound changes in the way we cook and eat. The design of the cooker has been revolutionised, along with attitudes towards cooking, the availability of ingredients and our ability to keep food fresh.

Fifty years ago, nearly all food was prepared at home from the basic ingredients – and it was not just main meals that were home-made, many people made their own bread. (Here is a golden opportunity to learn through cooking, as the making of bread from scratch is an excellent means of giving children an insight into the past. [See page 24 for details.] A visit to the baking unit of a local supermarket would also be helpful.) Much of the food that was not home grown came from local sources. Fruit and vegetables only came in season, except for bananas and oranges.

Fifty years ago there was also mass immigration into the UK following World War II, when people from all over the Commonwealth arrived to find that staple ingredients they had used in cooking every day in their native country were rare or completely unavailable here. They were forced to improvise and create new dishes.

All cultures and families have different traditions related to food, different methods of cooking and eating – and all of these can be brought to life for children by their parents, grandparents and great-grandparents. Talking about food and preparing it together is rich with opportunities to learn about history and cultural history.

Physical development and movement

Physical skills from cooking sessions are developed when children have sufficient time and space to use a range of equipment in a safe and comfortable environment. They soon discover that some activities – such as mixing or rolling out pastry – are easier to carry out if they are standing up, or that they may need someone to hold a bowl while they whisk its contents. When making pastry children learn the need to use the tips of their fingers for the rubbing-in process and not their palms. They learn how to roll out the dough to a suitable size and thickness and to cut out shapes close together to maximise the number produced. All this experience develops ideas of size, volume and area.

In cooking, children are given the opportunity to use equipment which develops specific skills, at first with adult support and then with increasing independence and ability. Practitioners need to plan their cooking area so that all children have access to it with appropriate equipment and heights of tables – if necessary to accommodate a child in a wheelchair, for example.

Cooking also provides opportunities for children to use and develop all their senses: seeing, smelling, tasting and touching ingredients to experience similarities and differences, and learning to distinguish the bubbling noise of boiling from the sizzle of frying. They can be encouraged to describe the properties of ingredients – sticky, runny, soft, hard, wet, dry, stretchy, squelchy, and so on – which increases and enriches their vocabulary.

Aesthetic/creative development

Children's creative development depends on a rich, stimulating learning environment and the support of sensitive and responsive adults. Children therefore need the opportunity to explore and experiment with different materials and their own ideas. Cooking can offer these opportunities in a meaningful and satisfying way.

They may, follow a basic recipe to begin with but then adapt or change it by adding different flavourings and/or colourings to foods such as cakes and biscuits. They can use an icing bag to decorate their cakes, shapes or sweets to make the finished product their own individual creation.

Children can explore the colour, texture, shape and form of ingredients such as fruit and vegetables, and learn to display and present them in an attractive, aesthetically pleasing way in salads or displays. They respond to what they see, hear, smell, touch and taste, and need the opportunity to discuss and comment on their findings.

Adults need to ensure that the children have easy access to good quality resources, stored and displayed attractively. They can act as role models, sharing enthusiasm and appreciation of the children's efforts. They need to talk to the children about the work, introducing the appropriate technical vocabulary and giving them the opportunity to talk to each other and plan future projects.

Children can make their own dough – preferably plain using white flour, or perhaps brown using wholemeal flour – to use in their imaginative play, or in displays after decorating it or cooking it.

The depth of children's creativity in their role play is increased when they have explored real-life cooking sessions and meal times, and have participated in them. If they have experiences on which to draw they can play much better at setting up a Chinese take-away or at holding a tea party for a princess, a feast for a monster, a picnic on the moon or a banquet at a Roman villa.

Extending skills and confidence

The enormous potential for cooking to help young children learn in all the curriculum areas is enhanced by the many opportunities offered to children to develop independence. Once familiar with cooking procedures children can make simple recipes, such as cakes, with very little help and support. They can organise their own bowls, spoons and ingredients from labelled containers, and follow a recipe in steps, especially when each instruction is given in words and symbols. They can even carefully break an egg with a fork and mix it in if needed. Adults may need to help at different stages – perhaps to check the temperature of the oven, put the cake in and set the timer – but children can do much on their own and can clear up, especially when they have had experience of cooking at pre-school, or in reception or infant classes, as well as practice cooking at home. They are able to work independently with confidence in their own time and space, with help available when required. Such activities might well be challenging but are nevertheless achievable, and offer real-life situations with a satisfactory and pleasing end.

In a school or early years setting practitioners need to know the children's abilities and only intervene when necessary or for safety reasons. Equipment must be accessible so that children can select tools, recipes and ingredients. An extension to cooking simple cakes independently is for the young chef to work with another child, demonstrate to a group the process of making the cake and record it in some way with drawings and writing. Children with this level of skill and independence need to be involved in planning their next cooking project with the practitioner.

It is essential to develop this experience and confidence through regular joint cooking sessions, led and supported by an adult, with plenty of hands-on experience.

Involving families

There is no doubt that the close involvement of parents in cooking with their children is hugely beneficial. In these days of fast foods and TV addiction, 'cooking' increasingly means putting pre-prepared food in a microwave.

To help bridge this gulf parents and carers can be invited to the pre-school, nursery, reception or infant class to participate in supervised cooking sessions and to introduce recipes and dishes they cook at home. This will also develop parents' confidence in their culinary abilities. Another route is to give the children the recipes of something cooked in the setting which can be made at home. Children can even teach their own parents what to do. Alternatively, recipes can be included in regular newsletters. Families should be invited to celebration lunches, barbecues and end-of-term picnics, and involved in preparing the food with their children. Giving families the opportunity to cook and eat together at enjoyable events is an excellent way to show how much fun it can be and just might help encourage family meals at home – with the TV turned off.

Parents can also be encouraged to help the children grow fruit and vegetables, where this is possible, and to accompany the staff and children on trips to supermarkets, fruit farms and garden centres. A further possibility is to seek out parents from all sections of a diverse community who might act as cooking role models, not only in preparing and cooking foods at the school, but also in showing other parents how they cook at home.

Adults who are very interested in food and cooking often reminisce about helping their mother or grandmother in the kitchen. Children develop a love of good food from a very early age, especially when they are given responsibility for manageable tasks and if their efforts are praised and appreciated.

Many celebrity chefs such as Nigella Lawson, Heston Blumenthal and Jamie Oliver promote the importance of involving children in every aspect of food preparation, of making it fun and helping children to understand what is happening and why. In *Happy days with the Naked Chef,* Jamie Oliver talks about going shopping with children and letting them choose, for example, a ripe melon or pineapple, the ingredients for a salad or fillings for sandwiches [see 'Further reading', p.30]. There are so many exciting ways in which children can help safely: making marinades and salad dressings; bashing spices in a pestle and mortar; picking herbs, smelling them and tearing them up; squeezing lemons; mashing vegetables; watching bread dough rise and decorating the tops of their own pizzas. Oliver stresses the importance of children having a wide, varied and healthy diet rather than junk foods such as fish fingers, burgers and chips, and gives several ideas for fun foods, including fruit-juice lollypops, frozen yoghurt, biscuits with soft chocolate centres and sticky toffee cupcakes. Children can make these for themselves, with a little help.

What practitioners can do

Growing fruit and vegetables

One of the most exciting and meaningful projects for children is growing their own food. A small chequerboard garden is ideal for this, as it gives access to squares of soil upon which can be grown salad vegetables, potatoes, carrots, tomatoes, marrows, beans, rhubarb, herbs, and so on. If a garden is not available, then grow-bags, tubs, boxes or trays can be used instead.

One such project involved the children in developing a strawberry patch in a nursery garden. There was great excitement when the first strawberries appeared and turned red. Not many made it inside the nursery, but an interest was developing into ways of using the fruit. It was decided to visit a fruit farm so that the children could pick their own strawberries. With the cooperation of parents and a very welcoming farm, a large group of children actually picked 25 kilograms of strawberries and several more of gooseberries, redcurrants and blackcurrants.

The next few days were spent preparing the fruit for jam making, ice cream, strawberry granita, milk shake, strawberry cakes, meringues and shortbread [see page 23–24 for recipes]. The children made bread on which to spread the jam and shared the other produce with their parents at the summer picnic. The children shared their work with their families and some made the recipes at home and visited the farm again with their families.

Growing potatoes is another involving project: the children love to see the shoots appear through the soil and then eventually dig out the grown vegetable. Making vegetable soup using these potatoes, along with marrows, courgettes, beans, onions and tomatoes is a very popular activity, and even children who are adamant that they hate soup enjoy it when they have made it themselves.

Tomatoes usually grow very successfully and, when ripened, taste and smell completely different to the ones bought in the supermarket. They can also be made into tomato soup and, even when green, into chutney and pickle.

Cook all the time

The most important thing that practitioners can do is to cook with children as often as possible. To do this successfully, it is vital to know a wide range of recipes using ingredients that are easy to obtain and to have a store of stock ingredients available at all times. In this way, practitioners can use cooking in planned activities to extend the children's interests and are also prepared to respond at short notice should the children request a cooking session.

The next chapter is full of recipes and ideas to cook with children throughout the school year.

Recipes for learning through the year

Spring

At the beginning of the year, when the days are short and the weather generally cold an initial emphasis on 'warming' recipes is appropriate.

At this time, try to make the children aware that even in January and February the sun has some power, which can be harnessed under glass, and that the renewal of spring is not far off. To do this plant seeds and leave them to germinate on the windowsills: sow cress on wet blotting paper and (in soil) sow lettuce, cabbages, beans, beansprouts and tomatoes. Since children are naturally impatient, cress and beansprouts are particularly popular, because they can be ready to eat – the cress in sandwiches, the beansprouts in salads or a stir fry – within a week. The other seedlings can be planted out in the garden at the end of term, just before Easter.

Lentil, carrot & celery soup

Method: Gently fry approximately 450g (1lb) chopped carrots and 1 head of celery in 3 tablespoons cooking oil in a saucepan. Add 110g (4oz) lentils – red, green or brown – and 1.2 litres (2 pints) stock, using stock cubes or powder. Boil for half an hour or until the lentils are soft. Liquidise and add 150ml ($1/4$ pint) milk, plus seasoning.

Learning opportunities: This recipe introduces the children to some less familiar but nutritious vegetables and other ingredients, and involves them in plenty of cleaning and chopping. The children are also able to see the lentils become soft and mushy during the cooking process.

When to make: Cold days at the end of winter and beginning of spring

Spaghetti alla carbonara

Method: Fry 4 bacon rashers cut into thin strips until crisp and add 100ml (4fl oz) cream. Beat 1 egg with 30g ($1 1/2$oz) cheese in a separate bowl. Cook the chosen pasta – for example, fettuccini, spaghetti, tagliatelle – in salted boiling water, drain and return to the saucepan with a knob of butter. Add the bacon and cream mixture, and toss; then add the egg and cheese mixture. Season, and sprinkle with grated parmesan cheese.

Learning opportunities: Most children in the UK will have heard of bacon and eggs and also of spaghetti. This is how the Italians combine the two to make a filling and warming dish – just the thing for a cold winter's day. The name of the dish can be turned into a chant for the children, particularly if there is an Italian child in the class to teach them the words.

When to make: End winter/beginning spring

Fried rice with fried mixed vegetables and prawn crackers

Method: Fry 1 finely chopped onion and a few mushrooms in oil in a saucepan. Add 450g (1lb) long grain rice and stir it into the vegetables. Pour in enough chicken or vegetable stock to just cover the rice, turn heat to very low and cover the pan tightly. Leave for half an hour before checking the rice. Peas, chopped spring onions, prawns, shredded ham, bamboo shoots and water chestnuts can be forked in as desired.

Learning opportunities: Here, many children will learn about vegetables which are unfamiliar to them, such as bamboo shoots and water chestnuts. Serve with chopsticks: the children love trying to use them and their attempts help to develop manipulative ability. Some can succeed surprisingly quickly. Any Chinese children in the class can be consulted over ingredients and involved in the preparation of this recipe (and others to follow). It will offer them a marvellous opportunity to be 'experts', especially when they can help their friends learn to use the chopsticks.

When to make: Chinese New Year

Fresh lychee and other fruit salad

Method: This simply requires the children to cut up a good deal of fresh fruit which is transferred to a large bowl. In addition to the better-known kinds of fruit such as apples, oranges and bananas, the fruit salad can include water melon, pomelo, rambutan, papaya, mango, mangosteen, custard apples or star apples. All go well with the lychees.

Learning opportunities: The preparation involves the children in a lot of shelling, peeling, de-stoning, chopping and dividing. Have them keep some pips and stones which can be planted in yoghurt pots full of soil. If these are placed in supermarket plastic bags and strung across the window, growth will be forced so that little lemon or orange trees appear in a matter of weeks.

When to make: Chinese New Year

Salad of beansprouts and other vegetables

Method: Mix beansprouts, baby corn, red pepper, mangetout, broccoli florets, button mushrooms and spring onions in a large bowl, chopping any ingredients which need it. Mix well. Any of the extra vegetables could be replaced with different ones. Mix and add a dressing such as soy sauce or olive oil and lemon.

Learning opportunities: More unusual vegetables here. Show the children that salad needn't just be a boring affair of limp lettuce.

When to make: After Chinese New Year

Pancakes for Pancake Day

Method: Beat together 100g (4oz) plain flour, 1 egg and 300 ml ($\frac{1}{2}$ pint) milk to make a batter. (This will make about 10 pancakes in a small frying pan.) If you can, allow the batter to stand for half an hour, then whisk to bring back to life. Heat vegetable oil in a frying pan, and ladle in enough batter for one thin pancake, tilting the pan to ensure that the batter covers it evenly. After a minute or so, lift the edge of the pancake to check that it is lightly browned, then turn it over with a palette knife or slice and brown the other side. Or you could toss the pancake, in traditional style. Repeat this method for each pancake, making sure to add new oil to the pan every time. Pancakes can be stacked one on top of the other, with a little sheet of greaseproof paper in between each to stop them from sticking. They can be served with sugar and lemon, jam or fresh fruit.

Learning opportunities: Helping to mix the batter and squeezing and cutting fruit gives the children plenty to do – and when the pan has cooled and the pancakes already made, they can have a go at tossing the pancakes themselves.

When to make: Shrove Tuesday

Carrot cake

Method: You will need two 20cm (8-inch) sponge tins. Grease the tins, and line the bases with greaseproof paper. Whisk together 175g (6oz) dark brown sugar, 2 large eggs and 150ml ($\frac{1}{4}$ pint) sunflower oil. Add 200g (7oz) wholemeal self-raising flower, 3 teaspoons mixed spices, 1 teaspoon bicarbonate of soda, mixing in gently, followed by 200g (7oz) coarsely grated carrots and 110g (4oz) sultanas. Divide the batter between the two tins and bake for approximately half an hour at gas mark 3, 170°C, 325°F. A syrup glaze, made from orange and lemon juice and brown sugar, can be poured over the cakes when they are still hot in the tins. When cold, they can be sandwiched together and covered in cream or a mixture of mascarpone and fromage frais.

Learning opportunities: This requires a good deal of peeling and grating, and introduces the children to carrots in an unusual culinary role. Keep some uncooked carrots so that they can compare the taste of raw carrots with cooked carrots.

When to make: March

Easter nests

Method: Melt 50g (2oz) butter, 4 tablespoons golden syrup and 100g (4oz) plain cooking chocolate. Stir in 75g (3oz) pulled-apart shredded wheat. Spoon into approximately 15 paper cases, putting a dip in the middle using a spoon, and allow to set in the fridge.

Learning opportunities: The melting and later solidification of chocolate teaches the children about physical changes of state. Shredded wheat forms the 'twigs' of the nest and eggs to be put in the dip can be made from icing sugar. To make these 'eggs' mix 1 egg white plus a few drops of chosen food colouring with a fork and gradually stir in sieved icing sugar to make a firm dough. Form into egg shapes and leave to dry out.

When to make: Easter. Make the nests during the last days of term, just before Easter, so that the children can take them home as gifts. As an alternative, chocolate crispy cakes can be made at any time of the year, with cornflakes or rice crispies added to the chocolate instead of shredded wheat.

Chocolate brownies

Method: Melt 375g (12oz) unsalted butter and 375g (12oz) dark chocolate into a pan. Beat 6 eggs with 500g (1lb) caster sugar and 1 tablespoon vanilla extract in one bowl. Into another, measure 225g (8oz) plain flour and 1 tablespoon salt. First beat the mixture of eggs and sugar and then the flour/salt mixture into the cooled chocolate mixture. Now add 300g (10oz) dried cherries or white chocolate chips or buttons, and beat again to combine. Scrape into a lined tin measuring approximately 33 x 23cm (13 x 9 inches), and 5.5cm (2 inches) deep. Bake at gas mark 4, 180°C, 350°F for about 25 minutes. Cut into squares when cool.

Learning opportunities: Lots of beating, and choices to make about what to add to the brownie mixture.

When to make: Easter

Hot cross buns

Method: You will need a greased baking sheet. Make the dough using 450g (1lb) plain flour, 1 sachet (7g) quick-action yeast, 1 tablespoon salt, 1 tablespoon mixed spice, 50g (2oz) sugar, 75g (3oz) currants and 50g (2oz) mixed peel. Make a well in the centre and pour in 150ml (1/4 pint) water, 40ml (1 1/2 fl oz) milk, 1 beaten egg and 50g (2oz) melted butter. Mix to a dough and knead it until smooth and elastic. Cover the bowl with cling film and leave for about an hour in a warm place to rise. Knead again and divide into approximately 12 round portions. Make a deep cross in each bun with a knife and leave again to rise under a polythene sheet. After about half an hour bake for around 15 minutes at gas mark 7, 220°C, 425°F. Mix 2 tablespoons sugar and 2 tablespoons water, and brush the buns with this syrup while they are very hot to make them nice and sticky.

Learning opportunities: There's another change of state here: the raising of the dough through the action of the yeast. Also, opportunities for division and decoration.

When to make: Easter

Cheese tarts

Method: Make the pastry: rub 50g (2oz) butter into 100g (4oz) flour, then mix in 4 teaspoons of water to make a dough. (For a more detailed description of the pastry-making method, see 'Picnic mini-quiches; page 23.) Roll out this pastry, then cut it into rounds using a pastry cutter and place them into a greased tart tray (a baking tray with dips in it). In a bowl, mix together 50g (2oz) grated cheese, 4 teaspoons milk, 1 egg and salt and pepper to taste. Pour a little of the mixture in each of the pastry tart cases. Bake at gas mark 5, 190°C, 375°F for 15 minutes.

Learning opportunities: This recipe brings together a range of familiar ingredients – pastry, cheese and eggs – and provides satisfying opportunities for cutting out circles of pastry to form pie cases which are then filled with the cheese mixture.

When to make: March/April

Gingerbread men

Method: Melt 75g (3oz) brown sugar, 2 tablespoons syrup, 1 tablespoon black treacle, 1 teaspoon ginger and 1 tablespoon water together in a pan, and bring to the boil. Add 95g (4oz) butter and $\frac{1}{2}$ teaspoon bicarbonate of soda, then slowly stir in 225g (8oz) flour. Form a dough with the mixture and, when it is cool enough to touch, mould it into a ball shape. Put it in the fridge for $\frac{3}{4}$ hour, then roll out the dough and cut it into shapes using a gingerbread man cutter (or any other interesting shape). Decorate with currants and cherry strips to make eyes, mouths and buttons, then bake at gas mark 4, 180°C, 350°F for 10–15 minutes.

Learning opportunities: The children love shaping the dough into men and decorating them with eyes, noses, mouths and buttons.

When to make: March/April

Summer

Many leaf crops that were planted early in the year will start to come into season in early summer. Later on, soft fruits such as strawberries and raspberries become available. They can be picked by the children and either eaten fresh or made into jam.

'Above-ground' spring vegetable soup

Method: Lightly fry a selection of vegetables which are grown above ground in oil or butter with chopped onions. Add stock before the vegetables brown, and simmer until tender. Liquidise and season, add milk or cream.

Learning opportunities: The lettuces, broad beans, cabbages and other vegetables planted in the school garden can be harvested and used to create a tasty soup. Point out to the children that these ingredients are 'above-ground' leaf vegetables, as opposed to the 'below-ground' root crops such as carrots and potatoes which appear later in the year.

When to make: April/May. (Below-ground vegetable soup [see page 26] can be prepared in the autumn term. Above-and-below ground soup consists, of course, of a mixture of vegetables grown in and out of the soil, and can be made at any time of year.)

Picnic mini-quiches

Method: For the pastry put 225g (8oz) plain flour in a bowl with a pinch of salt. Add 110g (4oz) fat (either butter, solid margarine or half butter/half lard) chopped into the flour. Rub flour and butter together with the fingertips until the mixture looks like breadcrumbs. Mix in about 3 tablespoons water, gradually, with a fork, to make the dough. If possible leave the pastry in the fridge in a plastic bag for half an hour to chill. Roll the pastry out and stamp out circles to line pastry or tart tins. To fill the tarts whisk 2 eggs with 200ml (7fl oz) milk. Put your chosen filling ingredients into the tarts, for example grated cheese, sliced tomatoes, strips of sliced ham, sliced mushrooms, chopped spring onions and/or finely sliced leeks. Pour on the egg mixture and cook the tarts for about 20 minutes at gas mark 6, 200°C, 400°F.

Learning opportunities: Again, the children are involved in making pastry and cutting it into small pie cases. Some of the quiches can be given meat fillings, others vegetable fillings, to suit all tastes and dietary needs.

When to make: May/June. Suitable for visits to zoos, playparks, *etc*. A successful picnic with young children calls for mild and dry weather but not a heatwave

Picnic bean salad

Method: Top and tail 450g (1lb) French beans, cut in half and cook in salted water for about 10 minutes. Chop a bunch of spring onions. Combine these and the French beans with the drained and rinsed contents of 1 tin sweetcorn and tins of a selection of beans – red kidney, butter, broad, cannellini, flageolet, haricot, pinto and black-eyed, for example. Make a dressing using olive oil, vinegar, crème fraîche and salt and pepper. Pour over while the cooked beans are still warm. Stir in some chopped parsley.

Learning opportunities: Children often say they do not enjoy salads, but here is an opportunity to introduce them to something which is highly nutritious as well as different. It is full of so many things, that it offers opportunities to try out the different ingredients, and see which they like and which (if any) they truly don't. The effort they put into its preparation may persuade them to eat it afterwards.

When to make: May/June

Picnic sandwiches

Method: One way to make sandwiches interesting is to use a range of breads and try a variety of different fillings. Most children enjoy the old favourites of jam, ham, cheese and tuna, but the possibilities for other fillings are almost endless.

Learning opportunities: Although sandwiches may seem too 'obvious' for any formal recognition, their preparation has lots of useful lessons for the children as it involves cutting, dividing, buttering, filling and assembling. The children can also be consulted on their favourite fillings – especially if they have discovered something which might be seen as unusual to others. Only some children, for instance, will have been introduced to pickles in cheese sandwiches. The children can also be invited to come up with ideas for new filling combinations which no one has tried. Some might be rather odd, but others may turn out to be great favourites. Try setting up a 'production line' and allowing the children to change places.

When to make: May/June

Strawberry granita

Method: Hull, rinse and dry 450g (1lb) strawberries and blend to a puree in a food processor or liquidiser. Add 175g (6oz) caster sugar and blend again briefly. Add 570ml (1 pint) water and 3 tablespoons lemon juice. Blend again and sieve into a bowl, rubbing the puree through. Freeze in a polythene freezer box for two hours initially. Mix with a fork every hour until ready to be served.

Learning opportunities: The preparation, refreshing taste and sparkling appearance of a granita made from soft fruits are often new experiences for children and serve as an introduction to other types of sorbet, such as lemon, orange or lime.

When to make: July. Granita is just one of many dishes that can be prepared from early soft fruit such as raspberries and strawberries. Included here are ice cream, jellies and shortbread, but other possibilities are tarts, mousse, sauce, lollies and juice.

Strawberry ice cream

Method: Prepare strawberry puree as above but without the water, then fold in 570ml (1 pint) whipped cream, and freeze.

Learning opportunities: The children are often surprised to learn that ice cream can be made at home – and be more delicious than any ready-made product.

When to make: July

Strawberry shortbread

Method: Mix 110g (4oz) plain flour with 50g (2oz) caster sugar, 50g (2oz) fine semolina and 110g (4oz) softened butter in a bowl with a wooden spoon to form a dough. Roll the dough into a fat sausage and put it in the fridge in a polythene bag for about 20 minutes. Slice the 'sausage' into approximately 16 thin rounds and place in greased tart tins. Prick each one thoroughly with a fork and bake for about 30 minutes at gas mark 2, 150°C, 300°F. Leave to cool on a wire rack. To serve, fill each tart with whipped cream or softened cream cheese mixed with crème fraîche and top with strawberries, dusting with a little caster sugar.

Learning opportunities: Another recipe involving a doughy mixture which the children can mix, knead, divide and shape into individual biscuits.

When to make: July

Strawberry jam

Method: For all jams and sweets, see *Jams, preserves and edible gifts* by Sara Paston-Williams [see 'Further reading', p. 30].

Learning opportunities: Although the preparation is brief, the boiling lengthy and the result – to be handled by adults only – hot, sticky and likely to burn, there are still lessons to be learned from the making of jam. Colours for instance: red, purple, deep purple; and the effect of heat over a long period on the consistency of a fruit/sugar mixture.

When to make: July. Pots of jam make a lovely gift for children to take home with them

---

Lemonade

Method: Wash 6 lemons in warm water and squeeze them, reserving the juice. Boil approximately 2.28 litres (4 pints) water with 150g (6oz) sugar and the lemon halves for 30 to 60 minutes. Allow to cool, add lemon juice and strain into bottles. Dilute with soda water or with traditional lemonade and ice-cubes.

Learning opportunities: Prove to the children that home-made fruit cordials can be altogether more delicious than any mass-produced fluid sold in a bottle.

When to make: Can be made for a one-off barbecue or in any period of hot weather

Autumn

Harvest time offers many wonderful opportunities for cooking

Quick bread rolls

Method: Set oven to gas mark 8, 230°C, 450°F. Put 350g (12oz) strong flour, 1/2 sachet (3g) quick-action yeast and a pinch of salt into a bowl. Add 1 dessert spoon vegetable oil and 210ml (7fl oz) warm water. Mix to form a firm dough. Put the dough on a floured table and knead for about five minutes. Shape into rolls and put on a greased baking tin. Leave in a warm place until the rolls have doubled in size, then bake for 15–20 minutes.

Learning opportunities: The raising action of yeast is only the most obvious lesson for children in the baking of bread. Try to put over the importance of bread in the growth of the world's civilisations. A display comparing breads and a session spent making and eating breads from all over the world can be very instructive and part of a harvest topic.

When to make: September/October

Rainbow jam session

Method: The methods for making a range of jams using a variety of fruit are available in *Jams, preserves and edible gifts* by Sara Paston-Williams [see 'Further reading', p.30].

Learning opportunities: The availability of a wide range of soft fruits, including blackberries, redcurrants, damsons, plums and greengages presents an opportunity to make, over several cooking sessions, a range of jams of widely differing colours. By extending the project to include marmalade and lemon curd, a sequence of jam jars can be built up of hues which include most of the primary colours in the spectrum: red, orange, yellow, green, blue, indigo, violet.

When to make: September/October

Plum tarts/apple pies

Method: For the pastry follow the recipe for mini–quiches [see page 22], adding 25g (1oz) caster sugar before the water. If making individual pies, fill small foil containers with the chopped raw fruit – such as apples, blackberries, cherries, plums, gooseberries or blueberries – and a sprinkling of sugar. Roll out the pastry and cut out a circle to cover and seal well. Cut two slits in the pastry lid and brush the surface with a little milk, sprinkling a little caster sugar on top. Bake at gas mark 5, 190°C, 375°F for 20–30 minutes.

Learning opportunities: Autumn soft fruit can also be eaten immediately, of course, but the preparation of a fruit tart provides plenty of tasks for the children: the washing, peeling, de-stoning and cutting of the fruit and, separately, the making of pastry dough which is then rolled into sheets to make the tarts and pies.

When to make: September/October

'Below-ground' harvest vegetable soup

Method: As for 'Above-ground' soup [see page 21].

Learning opportunities: Late-harvested root vegetables such as carrots, onions, potatoes, parsnips and turnips can be brought together to create a tasty and health-giving soup.

When to make: October

Pumpkin muffins

Method: Cream 110g (4oz) butter or margarine until soft. Add 175g (6oz) brown sugar and 110g (4oz) black treacle, and beat until light and fluffy. Add 1 beaten egg and 225g (8oz) cooked pumpkin flesh, and stir until well blended. Lightly fold in 200g (7oz) sifted plain flour, a pinch of salt and 1 teaspoon each of bicarbonate of soda, ground cinnamon and grated nutmeg, plus 50g (2oz) currants or raisins until just evenly combined. Spoon the batter into approximately 14 greased muffin tins or paper cases until about two-thirds full. Bake for 12–15 minutes at gas mark 6, 200°C, 400°F.

Learning opportunities: Children will be fascinated to discover that the not-very-appetising interior of a pumpkin can be scooped out to make these delicious muffins. Afterwards, of course, the tough external skin of the pumpkin can be used to make a Hallowe'en lantern.

When to make: Hallowe'en

Pumpkin, coconut and sweetcorn soup

Method: Fry chopped onion gently in butter and olive oil, adding the chopped, peeled flesh of a medium pumpkin (or squash) and 1 diced potato. Cover and cook gently for about 15 minutes. Add stock and simmer gently until soft. Cool, add 1 tin coconut cream or milk and a tin of drained sweetcorn. Liquidise, add salt and pepper and milk to taste and reheat gently. Sprinkle with chopped parsley or chives.

Learning opportunities: The rather bland squash vegetables can be the basis for delicious soups when combined with other flavours.

When to make: Hallowe'en

Bonfire toffee and parkin

Method: For bonfire toffee, see *Jams, preserves and edible gifts* by Sara Paston-Williams [see 'Further reading', p. 30]. For the parkin, pour 200g (7oz) syrup and 25g (1oz) black treacle into a saucepan and add 110g (4oz) margarine and 110g (4oz) soft brown sugar. Melt over a gentle heat. Put 225g (8oz) oatmeal, 110g (4oz) self-raising flour and 2 level teaspoons ground ginger into a bowl and thoroughly stir in the warmed syrup mixture. Add 1 beaten egg and 1 tablespoon milk. Pour the mixture into a 20cm (8-inch) greased square cake tin and bake at gas mark 1, 140°C, 275°F for 1½–2 hours. Cool completely in the tin before turning out and keep for at least a week before eating.

Learning opportunities: Two popular sweetmeats to eat while the fireworks go off. There is a change of state to observe when the mixture of butter and sugar turns into the hard toffee that can be broken with a hammer, while the parkin – a form of gingerbread – is easy to make.

When to make: Bonfire Night

Winter

This season is, of course, full of opportunities for recipes which help celebrate mid-winter festivals. Here are some recipes which fit that bill. Many of the early spring recipes are also appropriate to make in November and December [see pages 17–20].

Samosas, cucumber raita and dal

Method

Samosas: These little savoury snacks can be stuffed with almost anything, but spicy potatoes, onions, peas or minced meat cooked with mint are traditional fillings. The thin circles of pastry can be bought ready to use. Cut each in half and form a cone, gluing the seam with a little water. Fill the cone with the chosen stuffing, closing the top with a little water. Press the top seam down with a fork. Heat 4–5cm (1½–2 inches) oil in a wok or deep frying pan until medium hot, and fry samosas in a single layer until golden brown and crisp.

Raita: Raitas are relishes or dips which can be made with fruit, vegetables and herbs. Beat 450ml (¾ pint) plain yoghurt lightly and add ½ teaspoon salt, ¼ teaspoon cayenne pepper (optional), and mix well. Fold in approximately 10cm (4 inches) finely chopped cucumber and 2 tablespoons chopped mint.

Dal: Dals can be made from red split lentils, whole green lentils, yellow lentils or yellow split peas. Combine 200g (7oz) lentils with 1 litre (1¾ pints) water and bring to the boil. Remove the scum and add a few thin slices of ginger and ½ teaspoon of turmeric. Simmer very gently for 1½ hours, stirring regularly towards the end to prevent sticking. Add salt to taste and remove ginger slices. Sprinkle chopped coriander on top to serve.

Learning opportunities: The children can be involved in the preparation of all these dishes which provide an experience of Indian food. Children who regularly eat these foods at home will be able to share their expertise with practitioners and the other children. A great deal of skill is needed to produce perfect samosas, but luckily – as long as the cones are sealed – they seem to survive the frying, so children with varying manipulative abilities will be successful in producing an acceptable outcome. Poppadums, poori [see below] and naan breads are very popular with children to dip in the raita and dal. Halva and other sweets such as gulab jamum and kheer can also be eaten in school and are very popular with the children. See *Madhur Jaffrey's Indian cookery* and *The Usborne round the world cookbook* [see 'Further reading', p. 30].

When to make: Diwali and Eid al Fitr at the end of Ramadan

Pooris (deep-fried puffed breads)

Method: Put 225g (8oz) chapati flour (or half wholemeal and half plain white flour) and ½ teaspoon salt into a bowl. Drizzle on 2 tablespoons groundnut oil and rub it in with the fingers. Slowly mix in enough water (approximately 90–110ml; 3–3½ fl oz) to form a soft ball of dough. Turn out on to a floured surface and knead until smooth. Rub ball of dough with a little oil and leave to rest in a covered bowl for 10 minutes. Divide the dough into 12 balls. Roll them into 13cm (5-inch) discs, keeping covered. Lay them one at a time on top of hot oil in a wok or frying pan. Hold each disc down gently as it puffs up, flip over and cook for a further few seconds. Keep on a plate lined with kitchen paper while the rest are cooked.

Learning opportunities: These are very popular with the children who can work on the preparation of the dough and breads up to the deep-frying stage. Dividing the dough into individual pieces, comparing and counting the resultant balls and then rolling them into discs are all tasks that provide the children with experience of area and conservation. The further expansion of the pooris as they are cooked causes great excitement. Pooris are lovely dipped into the raita.

When to make: Diwali and Eid

Potato latkes

Method: Grate 700g (1½lb) potatoes. Drain in a sieve. Separately mix half 1 coarsely chopped onion, 1 egg, salt and pepper and 1–2 tablespoons self-raising flour or matzo meal. Add the grated potatoes and mix until pulpy – this can be done briefly in a food processor and should create a thick, sticky mess. Add more flour if at all runny. Fry the latkes in lumps of about a tablespoon in hot oil that is 1.25cm (½ inch) deep for about five minutes each side.

Learning opportunities: For the latkes the children can help with the peeling and grating of potatoes and the creation of a batter. From a safe distance they can then watch the formation of the latkes as the batter is dropped into hot oil.

When to make: Hanukkah

Small Christmas puddings

Method: To make 16 mult 175g (6oz) puddings …

Stage 1: Mix the dry ingredients together in a large bowl. These are: 227g (8oz) shredded suet (low-fat vegetable suet can be used), 110g (4oz) sifted self-raising flour, 225g (8oz) white breadcrumbs, 2 level teaspoons ground mixed spice, ½ teaspoon freshly grated nutmeg, a good pinch ground cinnamon, and 454g (1lb) soft dark brown sugar. Add 1kg (2lb 2oz) mixed dried fruit and 50g (2oz) mixed peel. Chop 2 small cooking apples and grate the zest of 1 large orange and 1 lemon. Stir into the mixture. Whisk 4 large eggs and add with 570ml (1 pint) mixed citrus fruit juices. This is a good time for all the children to have the opportunity to stir the mixture, experience the spicy smells and make a wish. The bowl should then be covered and left overnight.

Stage 2: The next day the mixture can be ladled into small foil pudding basins and covered with greaseproof paper and foil. The puddings can then be steamed for three hours. A slow cooker is very useful for this job. Once cool, the puddings can be stored and decorated to take home as gifts. Another hour of steaming will warm them up when required

Learning opportunities: This recipe has everything: weighing, measuring, counting, mixing, stirring (and making a wish), apportioning (to create a set of small puddings) and decorating. It has to be done in two or three sessions, but that makes it easy for the whole class to be involved. It also provides cultural learning opportunities for children who have not grown up in British homes. Some children in pre-schools from different cultural backgrounds will be young enough never to have experienced these flavours. Here, culturally British children can be cast as experts in passing these experiences on.

When to make: Just before the Christmas break: the children can take home the small puddings as gifts.

Marzipan petit fours and fondant icing sweets

Method: Marzipan and fondant icing can be bought ready-made, rolled out on a surface, sprinkled with icing sugar and cut into shapes using small sweet cutters. They can also be moulded by hand into shapes, placed in small paper cases and decorated with tiny sweets, bits of angelica or glacé fruits, grated chocolate or hundreds and thousands.

Learning opportunities: Rolling, moulding, shaping and cutting marzipan or fondant icing are very satisfying and pleasurable activities for children which demand care and dexterity. There are opportunities for children to develop and exercise their creative skills in the decoration and display of their efforts and they take pleasure in producing a gift they have made themselves.

When to make: Christmas

Quick Christmas cake

Method: In a large bowl mix together 450g (1lb) mincemeat, 225g (8oz) wholewheat flour, 3 level tablespoons baking powder, 150g (6oz) dark brown sugar, 150g (6oz) softened butter or soft margarine, 175g (6oz) mixed dried fruit, 50g (2oz) chopped walnuts, grated zest of 1 orange and 1 lemon, and 3 eggs. Spoon the mixture into a 20cm (8-inch) lined and greased cake tin, and bake for about 1 hour 20 minutes at gas mark 3, 170°C, 325°F.

Learning opportunities: Traditional Christmas cake is complicated but this short-cut recipe provides plenty of involvement for the children while being simple to make. It provides an opportunity for the children to follow a recipe, possibly through symbols, ticking off each ingredient as it is added. New skills can also be taught, including zesting the citrus fruits, breaking the eggs and mixing together the many ingredients. During preparation and cooking the children will notice the unusually rich smells which are associated with Christmas cooking. They will enjoy decorating their cakes, perhaps with a snow scene, traditional figures or trees and then sharing the results with families at the end of term party.

When to make: Christmas

Further reading

Cookery books aimed at children

Irvine, P. (2001) *Easy peasy all the time,* London: Ebury Press.

Peebles, L. (1991) *We can cook,* London: Ladybird.

Millard, A. (1993) *The Usborne round the world cookbook,* Tulsa: Oklahoma, Educational Development Corporation.

Morris, A. (1993) *Bread, Bread, Bread,* New York: William Morrow.

Walden, H. (2000) *The great big cookie book: over 200 recipes for cookies, brownies, scones, bars and biscuits,* London: Lorenz Books.

Other good cookery books

Blumenthal, H. (2002) *Family Food: a new approach to cooking,* London: Michael Joseph.

Jaffrey, M. (1982) *Madhur Jaffrey's Indian cookery,* London: BBC.

Oliver, J. (2001) *Happy days with the Naked Chef,* London: Michael Joseph

Paston-Williams, S. (1999) *Jams, preserves and edible gifts,* London: National Trust.

Smith, D. (1995) *Delia Smith's book of cakes,* London: Coronet.

Best-kept secrets of the Women's Institute series

Brand, J. (2003) *Home Cooking,* London: Simon & Schuster.

Cook, S. (2003) *Chocolate,* London: Simon & Schuster.

Herbert, L. (2003) *Tarts,* London: Simon & Schuster.

O'Regan, C. (2003) *Breads and baking,* London: Simon & Schuster.

Stories for children

Ashley, B. (1990) *Cleversticks,* London: Picture Lions.

Browne, E. (1997) *Handa's surprise,* London: Walker Books.

Chamberlain, M. & Umanksy, K. (1998) *Pass the jam, Jim,* London: Red Fox.

Cooper, H. (2002) *Pumpkin soup,* London: Doubleday.

Holmelund, E. & Sendak, M. (1982) *Little bear stories,* London: Mammoth.

The little red hen – traditional tale available in several forms, *eg* Randall, R. & Dodd, E. (2003) *The little red hen (touch and feel),* London: Ladybird.

Wood, D. & Wood, A. (1984) *The little mouse, the red ripe strawberry and the big hungry bear,* Swindon: Child's Play.

Yates, I. & Lewis, J. (1999) *The enormous turnip (first favourite tales),* London: Ladybird.